A LETTER TO MY YOUNGER
SELF UNMASKED

Ashley N. Thomas

Published by
Greater Working Women Publishing, LLC
www.gwwpublishing.com

Providing Publishing Services for Christian Authors & Organizations: Hardbacks, Paperbacks, E-Books & Audiobooks.

A Letter To My Younger Self Unmasked

Copyright © 2018 Ashley N. Thomas

All rights reserved. Printed in the United States of America. No part of this book may be used or reproduced in any manner whatsoever without written permission except in the case of brief quotations em-bodied in critical articles or reviews.

ISBN: 978-1-948829-02-1

First Edition: March 2018

Despite the pain, you have to get up and live your dream.

~Ashley

INTRODUCTION

It's necessary for each of us as women to do the essential work in our lives so that we can forgive ourselves, forgive others, and heal. It starts with revisiting and paying homage to the little girl that lives deep within our souls. Desperately yearning to be set free.

I've learned it is always God's desire for us to go and share our stories, whether we want to or not. God never wastes our pain. Only we as humans do that. God has a plan for a great purpose and a beautiful future for all who believe in Him. Not despite our past, but because of it.

So, I found the courage and the desire to turn my past pain into my purpose because when I realized I had the power to be victorious, I no longer wanted to be a victim. Well, what is it that you may need to say to your younger self? As you prepare to turn the page, I pray that the transparency, courage, and vulnerability I share is an inspiration to all.

Your scars tell a story. They are a reminder of when life tried to break you but failed.

~ Ashley

A LETTER TO MY YOUNGER
SELF UNMASKED

Dear Ashley,

If you are reading this, just know I needed to step back in time to write this letter to you. I am writing to you as your 29-year-old self, to reclaim the orphaned part of you. In all honesty, I am still you, just a little older and wiser of course. I know you have so many questions to ask and you'll want answers to a series of events that took place in your life. I promise to do my best to give you understanding, peace, and closure.

Ashley, your past played a significant part in your future. I can start in many places, but I choose to start at this particular moment in time because this was a time you needed me more than ever and I am sorry for not being there. At age five you were just learning to discover what life was all about and how you would fit into it! Exploring and getting in everything. Asking questions, curious, playing with dolls, and trying to find your place in this vast world. Instead of just living, a happy 5-year-old life your cousin decided to violate you. I now know that this was the most significant trauma you would face as a child during the crucial parts of your developmental and intellectual stages. This event would be just the beginning of the silencing of your voice. I want you to know that it was not your fault that you were molested and introduced to sexual things far higher than your small mind could begin to understand. It was not your fault that your cousin treated you like a porn star. Baby girl it was not your fault, for you were just an innocent 5-year old little girl.

In Pre-K, you often let a little boy put his hand in your panties at naptime, and you would do the same to him. You remember the time you were playing hide and seek with your other cousin, and underneath the table, he started touching on you? It was not your fault that you let him do it. You see it was not your fault because the trauma you experienced early on made you feel and think as a child, this was okay and that this was supposed to happen to you. It was not your fault that when they discovered the two of you, you were whooped with a belt until you bled. It was not your fault that no one asked you what happened. It was not your fault that the one man that was supposed to protect you completely stole your entire voice in that one moment. It was not your fault that instead of them listening to or educating you, they disciplined you. Do you see the pattern here Ashley? It was not your fault; you were living with the impact of your 5-year-old trauma.

You were just an innocent child battling demons that this cold world introduced you to at such a young age.

During that time of your life, you lacked intimacy, which affected how you functioned with emotional intimacy. Not having a childlike introduction to your developing body left you vulnerable to being touched inappropriately. A sexual toxic poison-tainted your intellectual stimulation. This poison is a nonmedical illness that will lead to needing medical help.

As you grew a little older, you begin to have some funny feelings for boys. I know you did not understand what these emotions and feelings meant and it is okay because had you been shown how to recognize or express your feelings you wouldn't have been confused.

You remember in the 4th grade when they were getting ready to introduce all the girls to something called a cycle. Well, you went home questioning about a period and that you needed someone to sign a paper so you could find out why they wanted all the girls to know about this crazy period thing. You were told to go back to school and say to your teacher that a period is a dot at the end of a sentence. You were so confused because you did not understand why they wanted to show all the girls about a punctuation you use every day in writing.

One Sunday morning you woke up with red stuff in your bed and panties. You panicked because you did not have a clue what, when, why, and how this happened. You went to the restroom to clean yourself, but the more you cleaned, the more red stuff appeared.

Being a woman unmasked means being completely naked. Not in the physical but stripped of all the things that made you become other than who you were born to be. It means being free to walk in your truth unapologetically. I AM proud to be a woman unmasked!

Although you were scared and did not know if you would get in trouble, you yelled for your mom to come. She cracked the door open, looked inside and you told her what was going on. She said, "Oh girl that's your period." Closed the door and came back a few minutes later tossing you a pad saying put this on. Still scared and confused, and left without an explanation about this situation.

Ashley, this is the "period" they wanted all the girls to know about at school. Your cycle is why you started to develop those funny feelings for boys. You were entering puberty love. At this time you needed to be emotionally connected to your mom for emotional comfort. You were growing into a young lady, and it was necessary to have support to ensure physical confidence. Due to the lack thereof, not only did you feel completely disconnected from your mom but also you felt manipulated which led to trust issues. Your dad needed to affirm your identity and physical beauty during this crucial time. Helping you understand your personality and the values you should live by throughout your life. The importance of being a good role model as well as choosing good friends and how to make the right decisions. You started to feel insecure and struggled with identity issues. You then masked yourself pretending to be something you were not. Know your dad loved you unconditionally and that it was not his fault, he developed an illness that temporarily took away his memory. It was not your fault that he no longer could be the man that you enjoyed traveling the world together.

At this point, your peers began to have a significant impact in your life. You wanted everyone to like you, and you desired to belong. You sometimes made poor choices, but it was not your fault. Ashley, you struggled with wanting to be the perfect child for your parents, but you also wanted to fit in at school. People only saw the outside and had no clue what you were facing on the inside. In your mind, you felt you did not have anyone to turn to, and you begin to live a double life, but again it was not your fault.

After being bullied and teased for wearing dresses and skirts all the time, you started to question your religion. You did not understand any of it and to be honest, it was never entirely broken down to you. Your faith and trust in God gradually died. You started sneaking wearing pants in hopes of being accepted. I understand your parents never noticed the effects of being taken from

Your power lies within the places you don't want to take people. Make your mistakes work for you and not against you.

private school to public school had on you. They never listened to you and expected you to just get over things. You felt so misunderstood because you were punished continuously and received whoopings for just trying to find your way through the crowd. Looking and searching for love. Wanting to be accepted for who you were.

You will grow up to feel helpless. You will be very angry and feel like a failure. It was not your fault that you were dealing with demons that were stronger than you were at the time. It was not entirely your fault that you got pregnant at 17. Had you been educated on sex by your parents and shown how to express yourself adequately, your voice wouldn't be silent, Ashley. Yes, you are a baby raising a baby while you are still developing. Yeah, this sounds pretty bad and trust me it is. You experienced a wide array of emotions and exposed to so much. I know this is the time you needed me the most and I hope you accept the fact that you did. Even after when this is all said and done, you will need me even more.

I know you do not feel fulfilled and accomplished. I know you are tired of the abuse and you are tired of getting into bad relationships. Being cheated on, lied to, and heartbroken. I understand being hit by your ex-wasn't pleasant and how he would say ugly things to you, but baby girl you need to continue to look and move forward. There is light at the end of the tunnel. The journey God has placed you on will push you to the limits where you want to fold and break. I want you to know Ashley you were the one built for such a time as this. A part of me thinks you knew this all along. On this journey, the rode will be bumpy and you will want to throw in the towel. Keep in mind some fantastic things are going to happen to you and through you. Yes, yes, yes! Queen, you will finish high school and college.

Without saying too much, you will discover the passion that draws you out of bed every morning. You will be the best version for your daughter. By the way honey, she is beautiful. Oh and guess what, you will start that business and will discover your voice. To top that, you will write that book. Yeah, I know you doubt all of this and think I am crazy, but you will see just watch! Most of all beautiful. you will discover that you're fearfully and wonderfully made from head to toe. Because of this, you will have the ability to give yourself effortlessly in everything that you do. All of this will become therapy for you. People will never forget the words you speak into and over their lives. There will still be times that you will get distracted and stop believing in yourself. Faith and God have never been your best friend, but they will be. All of this sounds far from the truth and does not make sense, for heaven's sake, I am your 29-year-old self who decided to take time to come back and visit such a beautiful, talented little girl. I promise one day when you read this letter you will understand better. You do not always have to be perfect and appear healthy. Being scared is okay. Queen, you will find so much strength in a foreign place. All those moments of fear, inadequacy, and vulnerability that you have been running from are the moments that will shape you to be the amazing woman that you are meant to be! You had to endure so much because your purpose was to overcome all the pain and to be the answer to a global problem.

Continue pushing because if you keep moving forward, you will be the key that unlocks the chains of those who are yearning to be free. Distractions are going to come left and right to keep you away from your purpose. People will interrupt your flow to get you off course. No matter what Ashley, just move forward baby girl. Protect your mind, ears, and eyes for they are your most valuable asset. Despite your circumstances, you will live your dream!

Love Always and Forever,
Your 29-year-old self

Remember... There's more to life than you think. Turn your pain into power.

ABOUT THE AUTHOR

Ashley N. Thomas is an entrepreneur, motivational speaker, and author. Not for one moment did her achievements come without sacrifice. Despite teen pregnancy, Ashley completed her education. Ashley has had the opportunity to share her story of trial and triumph as an entrepreneur, woman, and a mother. Her love for speaking continues to grow stronger and allows her to provide strategies for empowerment and productivity to teens, young adults, and women nationwide. She specializes in restoration and revitalization of youth and young adult women that have experienced traumatic life events such as teen pregnancy while offering tactical guidance of how families can navigate their path toward success. She currently resides in Houston, Texas with her daughter A'talia Nicole. Ashley has a passion for inspiring and reminding women, *despite your circumstances you can still live your dream*.

Visit www.Ashley-Thomas.com.